HEADLINES

REAL BUT RIDICULOUS SAMPLINGS FROM AMERICA'S NEWSPAPERS

COMPILED BY JAY LENO

WITH PHOTOGRAPHS BY GARY BERNSTEIN AND CARTOONS BY BOB STAAKE

TIMOTHY A WELCH

WARNER BOOKS

A Warner Communications Company

This book is dedicated in loving memory to Jerrold H. Kushnick
and Samuel Jared Kushnick

Copyright © 1989 by Big Dog Productions, Inc.
All rights reserved

Warner Books, Inc., 666 Fifth Avenue, New York, NY 10103

 A Warner Communications Company

Printed in the United States of America
First Printing: December 1989
10 9 8 7 6 5 4 3 2 1

Library of Congress cataloging in Publication Data

Headlines / compiled by Jay Leno.
     p.   cm.
  ISBN 0-446-39136-0
  1. Newspapers—Headlines—Humor. 2. American wit and humor.
I. Leno, Jay.
PN6231.N6H4 1989   89-22713
081—dc20   CIP

Cover design by Jackie Merri Meyer
Cover photo by Gary Bernstein
Book design by Giorgetta Bell McRee

INTRODUCTION

"Obviously, a man's judgment cannot be better than the information on which he has based it."

—Arthur Hays Sulzberger

The reason these headlines appealed to me is because they were never intended to be funny in the first place. That they're checked and rechecked by a proofreader makes them funnier still. Sometimes the humor is tinged with disbelief. I'll pick up my family newspaper, for example, and see the headline, "CONDOM INDUSTRY SLOW AFTER BIG GROWTH," and wonder, "Am I the only person in the world who noticed that?"

In this book we've deliberately avoided using headlines from tabloid or so-called "pulp" newspapers because the double entendres found in them are often intentional. It's when they're not but show up anyway in the local gazette, that you have to laugh. In the same way that a joke is funnier in church, a silly headline seems even sillier when it appears in a respected "organ of the people."

I'd like to thank the viewers of *The Tonight Show* who contributed the headlines that appear here and have made it possible for me to donate all author proceeds to charity. To them and to all of you who are encountering these headlines for the first time: Enjoy the laughs!

Jay Leno
New York, August 1989

1

One advantage a newspaper reader has over someone who watches television or listens to the radio is his ability to go directly to the stories that catch his eye—those stories that contain the most pertinent information. A good newspaper will offer not just information on the events of the day, but also...

LITTLE-KNOWN FACTS

Screwdrivers were made to tighten, loosen screws

Although it appears that one or two screwdrivers should be enough for a household without any confirmed do-it-yourselfers, even the unhandiest of families needs several of them.

Liquor sales dip blamed on less drinking

③

Criminal groups infiltrating pot farms

Criminal groups involved with drugs?
Is nothing sacred?

Researchers call murder a threat to public health

How long did this study take? Do you think it was more than ten minutes?

5

Bush gets briefing on drought; says rain needed to end it

This is the kind of no-nonsense, put-your-reputation-on-the-line problem-solver we need in the White House.

Living together linked to divorce

'Nuff said.

Boys Cause As Many Pregnancies as Girls

?

Some students walk others ride to school

Think this was a slow news day?

Tribal council to hold June meeting in June

Cherokee Nation of Oklahoma Tribal Council will hold its regular June meeting at the Jay Community Building at 9 a.m., Saturday, June 11. Following the coun-

Yes, but when is the August meeting?

DEATH ENDS FUN

Kinda says it 'all, doesn't it?

HIGHLIGHTS

12:01 a.m. ⓫ **1988 Crusade for Children**

Annual fund-raiser to benefit handicapped children in Kentucky and Indiana. (Continues until it ends.) ←

Unless, of course, it's over sooner.

Toxic waste tour planned

LANSING — A citizens group began a tour of Michigan on Monday to visit some of the state's worst toxic waste sites

W·I·N·T·E·R
ESCAPES

Las Vegas air & hotel ... From $199.00
Cancun air & hotel .... From $399.00
Mazatlan air & hotel .. From $299.00
Orlando air only .... from $179.00
Jamaica air & hotel .. From $319.00
→ **Chicago** air & hotel ....From $199.00

If you choose Chicago, may I suggest Wacker Drive?

(15)

Hope it doesn't rain!

3

In the last few years there's been a perception that Americans are soft on crime, that we're coddling criminals, that we're not dealing with them harshly enough. This next set of headlines may dispute those claims...

CRIME AND PUNISHMENT

Police use tear gas, SWAT team, battering ram, stun gun to oust woman, 65

What would they have done if her father was at home. They would have needed a tank!

'Shoot to stop' ordered for fights

And if that doesn't work, try talking to them.

Window found open

Warrenton police are investigating an attempted breaking and entering which occurred Thursday at the Animal Care Clinic at 657 Falmouth St.

When Officers ████████ and ████████ responded at 4:11 a.m. after an alarm went off, they found a rear window had been partially pried open, said Chief ████████.

No one was at the scene, nor was access gained to the building, he said.

Boy, there's nothing like old-fashioned police work.

Cockroach Slain, Husband Badly Hurt

Reuters

Tel Aviv

An Israeli housewife's fight with a stubborn cockroach put her husband in the hospital with burns, a broken pelvis and broken ribs, the Jerusalem Post newspaper reported yesterday.

This sounds like the plot of a Japanese monster movie.

Slayings put end to marriage

You think it's the cockroaches again?

"First step on that long road to rehabilitation" department:

Man admits killing violated probation

A city man found guilty of a 1984 execution-style murder admitted in federal court Tuesday that the conviction violated his 1983 federal probation on a drug charge.

Animal unit seeks rabbit witnesses

Gee, don't you think *one* rabbit witness would be enough?

City outlaws giving out phone numbers, addresses of police

Solves the problem of trying to find a cop when you need one.

"I don't know how they're getting back on the streets" department:

Jail's $34-million price tag doesn't include cell doors

Associated Press

JACKSONVILLE — A $34-million contract to build a new five-story jail lacks one major item — cell doors.

"It sounds to me like we're buying a car without the two front wheels. I thought when we voted to go ahead with the jail that it would come complete with doors," City Council member ████████ said Thursday.

④ Do you think you can get something for nothing? Are you always looking for a free lunch? Do you believe you can get more than what you pay for? Here are some bargains that will force even the most jaded to exclaim:

WHAT A DEAL!

STATE FARM

Auto
Life Fire

INSURANCE

FREE FLY SWATTER

Get Ready For Summer Now! Just For Calling And Comparing
Our Rates You Receive A FREE Fly Swatter!

Like A Good Neighbor
STATE FARM
Is There

Reprinted from Design News, Feb. 2, 1989 © Cahners Publishing Co.

Design a safe nuclear power plant and win $500.   Page 24

Here's a way to earn extra money in your spare time.

Step into
joyce

Genuine fake eelskin

Don't be fooled.
Accept only imitations.

AMERITECH PAGESPLUS • COUPON

FREE DINNER
WITH ANY PEST CONTROL JOB
ARAB TERMITE & PEST CONTROL
FREE SCHELDE'S GIFT CERTIFICATE — $5 VALUE
ON ANY JOB OVER $50.00
$10.00 VALUE ON ANY JOB OVER $150

NORTH
363-9061
SOUTH
455-6849

(LIMIT ONE PER CUSTOMER)

OFFER EXPIRES 12-31-89

Boy, my mouth is watering already...

MISSISQUOI CONSTRUCTION CO

Custom Homes   FmHA Homes

We use real nails

This is the guy who should be building that nuclear power plant. He uses real nails!

64" MICRO-MINI BLINDS

$3.99 ea.

23/26/27'' Wide!

64'' long vinyl sleek ½'' micro-mini blinds offer greater privacy when closed; breathtaking view when open White, Ivory Ready to hang. Incredible savings

A breathtaking view? Good, I'm tired of looking at that dumpster.

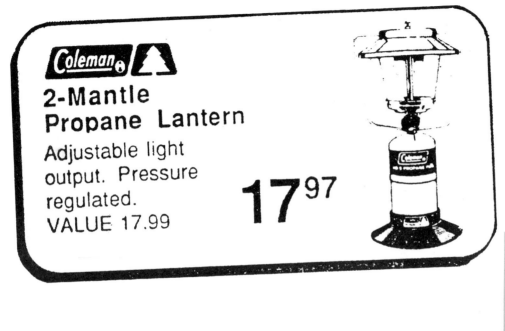

Coleman

2-Mantle Propane Lantern

Adjustable light output. Pressure regulated.
VALUE 17.99

17⁹⁷

Gee, why not buy two and save 4¢.

Petland ALIVE

PUPPIES & KITTENS

LARGE SELECTION OF AKC and CFA REGISTERED
VETERINARIAN CHECKED AND PETLAND
GUARANTEED— YOU ADD THE LOVE!

- Schnauzer
- Cocker
- Maltese
- Yorkie
- Shih Tzu
- Afgan
- Cairn
- Dachsund
- Lhasa
- Bichon Frise

- Siamese
- Oriental Short Hair
- Himilayan

The first rule of merchandising: convince the buyer that your product is superior to the competition. For example, notice that this store is selling *alive* puppies and kittens.

MINI-BLINDS

TRIPLE DISCOUNT SALE -- CALL NOW!!

TAKE OUR SUPER **70%** Off

THEN TAKE BONUS **+20%** Off

FINAL TRIPLE DISCOUNT **+10%** Off

YOU WON'T FIND A COMPARABLE BLIND AT A LOWER PRICE . . . GUARANTEED!!!

Hmmm...
100% off.
But does it have
a breathtaking
view?

New
math?

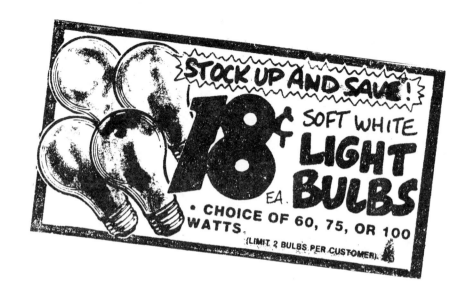

STOCK UP AND SAVE!

78¢ EA. SOFT WHITE **LIGHT BULBS**

• CHOICE OF 60, 75, OR 100 WATTS.

(LIMIT 2 BULBS PER CUSTOMER)

Rather than make two trips of one bulb each, why not stock up?

CLUB CAR GRILL

Our Reg. Steak
SANDWICH

2 for only $2⁹⁹
(Ingredients extra)

Hey, weight watchers, without the ingredients it's zero calories.

39

White Flower
Two Day Sale

FRIDAY ONLY

"Boy, am I hungry" department:

BUY ONE
GET ONE FREE
14 lb.
CHEESEBURGER

1 Coupon
Per Customer
Per Visit.

This coupon
not valid with
other specials.
With Coupon.
TVF.
Offer Ends
2/28/87

Ralston Muesli is <u>so</u> good, we guarantee you'll like it. We support our claim with a FREE box of Muesli!

Dear Ralston:

I didn't enjoy it. Thank you for sending me more.

Yours truly,
Jay Leno

42

The best things in life are FREE and here's how to get them!

SEND CHECK OR MONEY ORDER TO:

HOME VALUE COUPONS

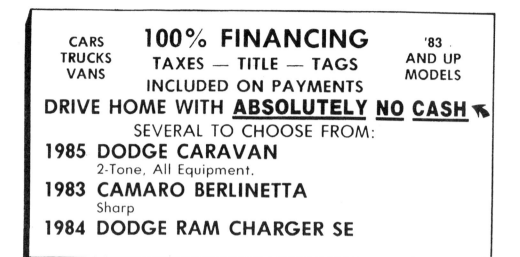

CARS
TRUCKS
VANS

100% FINANCING
TAXES — TITLE — TAGS
INCLUDED ON PAYMENTS

'83
AND UP
MODELS

DRIVE HOME WITH **ABSOLUTELY** <u>NO CASH</u>

SEVERAL TO CHOOSE FROM:

1985 DODGE CARAVAN
2-Tone, All Equipment.

1983 CAMARO BERLINETTA
Sharp

1984 DODGE RAM CHARGER SE

I like a guy who says what he means.

"Nutri/System, you lightened my life!"

Delicious food and personal counseling, helped ████████ lose 50 lbs. on the NUTRI/SYSTEM® Weight Loss Program.

The NUTRI/SYSTEM comprehensive *Flavor Set-Point*™ Weight Loss Program includes:

- *Personalized Weight Loss Profile*™ to identify your personal weight loss problem.

- A variety of delicious meals and snacks.
- One-on-one personal counseling.
- *Behavior Breakthrough*™ Program for long-term success.

Our client, lost 50 lbs.

Don't Wait, Call Today.

Of course she lost weight. They cut her hand off! She can't feed herself!

1 SOUND AND THE TIME PROJECTS ON THE CEILING
No need to turn on a light, squint your eyes, wake the
spouse. In fact, all you need to do is just cough, clap
your hands, whistle, speak...and our sound-activated
clock projects the exact time on your ceiling! Features
alarm and hourly chime mode; easy-read LCD display.
4"x3". Batteries not included. Assorted, let us choose.
G531491 — Clock.................... ~~$15.99~~; SALE $9.88

And what is your spouse doing while you're coughing,
clapping your hands, whistling, and speaking?

First they cut off their hands, then they shrink them!

Let Nutri/System help get you ready for the Holidays!

▬▬▬▬▬▬ lost 30 pounds and 25½ inches.

"It was the easiest program I've ever been on. It works!"

"Thanks Nutri/System"

47

FORECLOSURE LISTINGS

Entire state of NJ available. Deal directly with owners. 5-8 months before auction. Call 201-286-1156

The entire state of New Jersey. What a deal!

5

As was stated at the beginning of this book, none of this material was gathered from tabloid-type newspapers that deal in lurid, sleazy, sensational headlines, e.g., ELVIS SEEN PLAYING POKER WITH DOG. No, our sources are ordinary newspapers—ones meant to be read by the entire family. So if you see Grandma drop her tea, Junior pick up a paper with a hole in it, or Mom complain because there's an entire section missing, the following headlines could be the reason why...

PLEASE CANCEL MY SUBSCRIPTION

PIECES OF ROCK HUDSON SOLD

CONSUMERS LOVE THE TASTE OF BOOGERS!

NOSE PICKING CONTEST

TREES CAN BREAK WIND

COOKIES AND CONDOMS

RANGER TEXT PEETERS

TOILET SEAT FIRMS SIT DOWN AND TALK

CONDOM WEEK STARTS WITH BANG

Condom Week starts with a cautious bang

In 1968, a California pharmacist recommended to then-Governor Ronald Reagan that the California public be educated on the use of condoms to halt the spread of sexually transmitted diseases.

The public education tradition continues. Today marks the first day of National Condom Week, and UI Student Health Services does not plan to let the week go by unacknowledged.

Condom plant pulls out; was there a leakage?

Albany blew it again!

A Japanese condom manufacturer actually planned to come to Albany.

Okamoto Industries, of Ibaraki, Japan did their homework on Albany, the Good Life City before enplaining for the U.S.

Condom firm stretches product line

Now, for the man who has everything, or at least thinks he does, there's Maxx, the condom that's 25 percent larger than most.

‘We may be addressing the ego for many men, but on the other hand, it may be the only way to get them to use condoms.’

— *Maxx creator David Mayer*

California motorists carefully clean up condom spill

CORTE MADERA, Calif. (UPI) — A box containing about 5,000 condoms fell off a truck and scattered over a busy freeway, halting two lanes of traffic for a half-hour, the California Highway Patrol said.

Cookies with condoms fail family-taste test

MILWAUKEE (AP) — A record store that sold fortune cookies containing miniature condoms as a joke failed to draw a laugh from officials in charge of the city's largest summer festival.

'Chitlin' truck loses load in Climax

By Climax Reporter

Chitterlings arrived a few weeks early for Swine Time when an accident occurred involving an 18-wheeler tractor trailer rig carrying about 2,000 pounds of livestock (mostly hog) intestines and body parts, which are used in pet food, and a car (unknown in make or model) Nov. 1 at approximately 9 p.m.

From the "Your mother always told you to wear clean underwear" department:

Leave trousers behind for single's party fun

Staff Writer
It's every man's nightmare —
you're at a party with beautiful
women, you feel well-dressed, but
suddenly you realize you're not
wearing any pants.

This dream came true for about
600 single people at the Lafayette
Hilton Ballroom last week, and it
wasn't as bad for the men as it
would seem. In fact, the third
annual Boxer Shorts and Mini
Skirts Party "For Singles Only"
was a big success.

Rangers to Test Peeters for Rust

Capitals Goalie Makes 1st Start Since Feb. 17 Tonight

Pete Peeters owns the classiest goaltending statistics in the National Hockey League. He also has a medical record that has kept trainer Stan Wong gainfully employed during this season of minimal injuries for the Washington Capitals.

Lebanese chief limits access to private parts

BEIRUT, Lebanon (AP) — The military chief and head of the Christian Cabinet moved to reduce the power of private armies Sunday by ordering a ban

From the "Hear no evil" department:

Scientists Note Progress in Herpes Battle; Ear Plugs Recommended

From Our Wire Services

Scientists are making progress in battling genital herpes, a viral infection that was chipping away at casual sex before AIDS came along.

In one recent vaccine trial involving 161 sexual partners of type 1 (which causes oral herpes, or cold sores), had some protection against type 2 infection.

One drug that has shown promise in treating existing herpes lesions is acyclovir, called Zovirax by manufacturers Burroughs-Wellcome. Ongoing studies of the drug's effectiveness and

Health Watch

Ear Plugs Plugged

Ear specialists have a vision of a new health fad, and they'll give you an earful on it.

who work with jackhammers or jet planes.

Overexposure to noise is the most common preventable cause of hearing loss in the United States, says the academy in a new booklet.

Constant exposure to busy traffic, loud office machinery or even fic can have the same impact, can a couple hours next to a cha saw or pneumatic drill.

For more information, tl leaflet, "Noise, Ears and Heari Protection," is available. Send stamped, self-addressed busine envelope to the academy at 11(Vermont Ave., N.W., Suite 30

Man accused of excessively 'passing gas'

Trees can break wind

Wind can be a major factor in increasing the heating bill in winter. A natural way to curb the wind is with trees used as a windbreak.

"Good thing he wasn't in the smoking section" department:

Gas smell diverts flight, but it was just passenger's pants

FORT MYERS, Fla. (AP) — The pilot of a Braniff Airways flight made an emergency landing and all 47 passengers slid down chutes after people smelled gasoline on board — but the odor was later traced to a man's pants leg.

Yellow snow studied to test nutrition

Associated Press

SAVAGE RIVER, Alaska — Biologist Mark ▬▬▬▬ leaned into a razor-sharp wind and struggled through crusted snow in search of yellow patches that one day may allow scientists to predict nutritional problems in wildlife.

Caribou scramble to escape the helicopter ferrying ▬▬▬▬ and wildlife technician John ▬▬▬ onto the frozen tundra in this remote section of Denali National Park.

Casting this way and that, ▬▬▬ ▬▬ and ▬▬▬ checked urine-stained snow that may have been left by the fleeing animals.

I don't know how hungry *you* are, but when it comes to good eatin'...

Toilet-Seat Firms Sit Down and Talk

Two companies that believe there may be a lucrative market in sanitary toilet seats have reached an agreement in principle to merge.

Sheldon Fun Days includes nose picking contest

SHELDON — Sheldon children will finally be rewarded for breaking the rules Saturday — right on Main Street.

"You Can't Do That In Sheldon" activites at 4 p.m. Saturday are apart of Sheldon Fun Days which starts Friday. They include a nose picking contest, squirt-gun fights, water balloons, and other misbehavior.

From the "It tastes even better than yellow snow" department:

Candy consumers love the taste of Boogers

Stratford, Conn.
by the Associated Press

Tom Berquist was sitting at the dinner table with friends talking about why children like vulgar things, when he came up with an idea for a new candy.

He named it Boogers.

Some Pieces of Rock Hudson Sold at Auction

Associated Press

New York

An auction of memorabilia and furnishings from actor Rock Hudson's Beverly Hills mansion brought in $216,452 yesterday, with fans bid-

Talk about owning a piece of the rock.

FREE

For Qualified Senior Citizens and Persons With Low Income

Spay/Neuter Service

This will cure Grandpa's friskiness...

6

Airline personnel are quick to point out that flying is the safest way to travel. They'll give you persuasive statistics that compare the number of accidents to the number of miles traveled. Many go so far as to say that flying is safer than walking. Well, that may be true but when is the last time you saw an insurance machine in a shoe store? No thanks...

I'LL TAKE THE BUS

Cow was his co-pilot

MANHATTAN, Kan.—A pilot who landed in a farm field and then blacked out as the plane hurtled along the ground toward a steep ravine says an 800-pound Hereford gave its life saving him and his three passengers.

"The cow saved our lives, no doubt," said pilot ~~Seth In~~ ~~~~.

The cow was hit by the plane, limped away and later died.

Sounds like a great movie...

Pilot was wearing blinders

KINGSBURY, N.Y. — A student pilot wearing blinders was at the controls of a plane that collided with another aircraft over the Adirondacks, killing five people, authorities said Monday.

Blinders! I'd rather have the cow as my co-pilot than this guy.

Engine falls off plane, lands safely at O'Hare

CHICAGO (AP) — A Boeing 737 jetliner "lunged" and lurched after one of its engines fell off shortly after takeoff yesterday, but the pilot safely landed the plane, and none of the 32 people aboard were injured, officials said.

So if you want to be assured of landing safely, sit on the engine.

Council acts to ban airplanes on city streets

The Louisville City Council took the first step Tuesday evening to stop pilots from using land in the city as an airstrip without prior approval from the council.

It's about time. How many times have you pulled into a parking space only to see a DC-10 sitting there?

Pilot's injuries minor after crash

Associated Press

MANASSAS — Officials say a single-engine plane leaving Manassas Airport today crashed near the airport, but the pilot suffered only minor injuries.

A federal aviation spokeswoman said the crash could have been caused by the wings falling off the experimental plane. Kathleen Ber-

Hey, hey, hey, I wouldn't jump to any conclusions.

7

For many, sports headlines are among the most exciting in the newspaper, touting the record-breaking home run, the tie-breaking basket, the 90-yard run for the touchdown. Far more commonplace, though, are the foul balls that go into the stands and clunk the peanut vendor, in basketball the elbow in the eye, and in boxing the always humiliating, "He slipped in his own vomit." And so, here are the headlines that make up our sporting heritage...

THE SPORTING LIFE

Skiing season opens in Iran

When I think of a skiing vacation. I think of three places: Vail...Aspen...Tehran.

Death in the ring: Most boxers are not the same afterward

Yeah, I hear some of them are actually smarter.

Prior to the game, Larry Smith was placed on the injured list for the third time this season due to a <u>strained right thing</u>.

According to his wife, his left thing is still functioning perfectly.

6th Annual Youth Fishing Derby Sept. 5

The 5th Annual youth fishing derby, sponsored by Fountainhead State Park, will be held Sept. 5 at Picken's Lake, Fountainhead State Park Area No. 3.

Registration will be from 8:30 to 9 a.m. and tournament fishing from 9 to 11:30 a.m. A picnic lunch will be at 12 noon.

Prizes will be awarded to three age divisions, 6-8, 9-11 ages of hotdog buns or one package of potato chips.

Entrants must bring their own bait and tackle. Youth must also be accompanied by parents or an adult guardian.

Participants must comply with all fishing regulations and must use a cane pole or rod and reel. No dynamite or electrical devices will be permitted.

Talk about taking all the fun out of fishing, huh.

Pool Tournament

Every Tuesday Evening
At
7:30 P.M.

Double Elimination
$2 Entry Fee

Grand Opening Postponed Until Further Notice

Where is it? No wonder it's postponed.

Crappie Derby set for March

Better wear old clothes.

Most players on injured reserve apparently are actually injured

It kinda takes away your faith in the game, doesn't it?

Ski areas closed due to snow

Well, let's hope it warms up soon, eh.

Lack of water hurts ice fishing

The best ice fishing is oc
curring in backwaters chan
nels that have enough wate
And there's not many i
northern Illinois.

Think how the fish feel...

8

In today's modern society with Mom working, Dad putting in extra hours, and the kids involved in extracurricular activities, family time together becomes more important. But how should that time be spent? That's what we'll be looking at in...

FAMILY FUN

MULE DAY

ENTERTAINMENT FOR THE ENTIRE FAMILY

- Syrup Making • Flea Market • Arts & Crafts • Cake Walk • Rooster Sailing • Pedal Power Tractor Pull for Children • Turkey Shoot with Sling Shot

You know, if we all thought for a minute, I think we could find a crueler way to torture that turkey.

And when the kids tire of that slingshot...

Saxon Arms

Badger™ *Great Family Indoor Fun!*

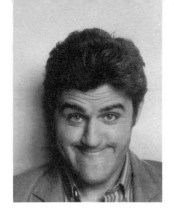

You want some gravy on your Nuprin, Ma?

NEXT WEEKEND DO SOMETHING SPECIAL FOR DAD

Take him for free tea and cookies at the garbage incinerator.

Next weekend there is a public Open House at the Lower Mainland's new—and first—refuse incinerator in Burnaby. You'll get a look at the plant to see how it works, receive a pin and other free handouts. And there will be entertainment—the magic of Imagination Market, children's shows, Rikki Recycle and more—coffee, tea, milk, juice and cookies. Free.

89

FATHER'S DAY SALE

Save 25-30%
All Lingerie

It's our semi-annual Foundation Sale! Stock up and save on our entire line of Bras, Briefs, Bikinis, Shapers and Daywear Coordinates for Women.

A. Reg. $16 **Sale $12.** Signature Collection underwire bra of nylon crepe. B, C cup.
B. Reg. $11 **Sale 8.25.** JCPenney seamless polyester contour bra.
C. Reg. $3 **Sale 2.44.** Tailored bikini of combed cotton. Sizes S, M, L. •
D. Reg. 2.75 **Sale 2.19.** Bright Vivana® nylon brief with cotton panel. Sizes S, M, L.

Shop our Fall Maternity Catalog for a great selection of comfortable fashions — from dresses to leisurewear.

LINE
CATALOG SHOPPING 1-800-

For that special dad who likes to dress up.

9

Did you ever read something and do a double take? You know you got it right the first time, but still, you go back and check anyway. Or to put it in layman's terms...

YOU WANNA RUN THAT BY ME AGAIN, PAL?

Ss. Peter and Paul to show pornography film

Ss. Peter and Paul Parish will sponsor a showing

I heard the church was getting more liberal, but this is ridiculous.

The Good News Announcer

How lovely on the mountains are the feet of him who brings Good News, who Announces peace, And brings Good News of happiness. Who Announces salvation, And says to Zion, "Your God Reigns!" Isaiah 52:7

"FOR, BY, AND ABOUT SOUTH FLORIDA CHRISTIANS"

Vol . 5 No. 5	Thanksgiving/Christmas 1988	$1.00

"By this all men will know you are My disciples, if you have love for one another." - John 13:35

THE END IS HERE!

What's the bad news?

93

Wisconsin bill would permit blind to hunt deer

From News staff

A bill overwhelmingly passed by the Wisconsin state legislature would allow blind people to roam the woods to hunt deer — provided they are accompanied by a guide to help point their weapons.

It's about time! This bill has been bottled up in the legislature long enough.

94

Man sues over mouse head in peanuts

Says he popped it in his mouth at an A's game; Coliseum is a defendant

Free mouse heads? Gee, when I was a kid all they had was Bat Day.

Eating dirt still a hard habit to break

LEXINGTON, Miss. — Emma Johnson tried hard to kick the habit. She took up smoking. She began eating laundry starch as a substitute. But the old craving still lingered.

I guess after a fast-food diet anything looks good.

Woman not injured by cookie

Staff Reporter

SARATOGA SPRINGS — A Saratoga Springs woman was not injured when she found a sewing needle in a Girl Scout cookie Thursday and wants to set the record straight.

Okay, she was lucky *this* time.

International Scientific Group Elects Bimbo As Its Chairman

Looks like Jessica Hahn may have a job after all.

Drought turns coyotes to watermelons

ATLANTA (AP) — Coyotes have a well-deserved reputation as chicken thieves, but in the dry year of 1988 they are also raiding south Georgia watermelon patches.

It's not the coyotes that bother me, it's those damn seeds.

Stop eating that
watermelon!

Pants Man to expand at the rear

Maurice "The Pants Man," the large-volume discount clothing store, will expand its Millbury Street main store with a two-story addition in the rear. Construction of the addition, which will face Harding Street, began several weeks ago and is expected to be completed by the middle of April, according to ~~Naugull Keeshan~~. a store official.

Furniture Drive for Homeless Launched

I'm sure that dinette set will look nice on Main Street, but shouldn't we be finding homes first?

Gerbil Selected Student Leader

NORWICH, England (AP) — A gerbil named Ken, campaigning on a platform of free beer and soft toilet paper, beat five other candidates to become president of the Student Union at the University of East Anglia.

It's amazing how the smartest ones always rise to the top.

FFA proposes name change to FFA

A proposed name change for the National Future Farmers of America organization has blessings from the current state FFA leaders, according to State FFA President Tim Teel.

The proposed amendment to the national constitution calls for the name to be changed from the National Future Farmers of America to the National FFA. It will be voted upon during the national convention, Nov. 10 to 12, in Municipal Auditorium, Kansas City, MO.

I guess the tough part is going to be changing all the stationery.

Dinosaur faces grand jury probe

Allegations of misconduct by public officials in the energy boomtown of Dinosaur are being investigated

The lawyer says his client will be extinct by the time the case comes to trial.

Man shot, stabbed; death by natural causes ruled

Associated Press

ROCHESTER — ███████ County Medical Examiner Dr. ███████ ███████ did not express shock or surprise that two of his investigators had ruled a 62-year-old man who was shot in the head and stabbed had died of natural causes.

"I don't think they were lackful, cavalier or something like that," ███████ said Tuesday. He called the mistake an "erroneous judgment."

■ Searchers find Big Ugly child

BIG UGLY, W.Va. — A child, who spent 17 hours

Family catches fire just in time, chief says

The Richard Harder family Sunday returned home from church just in time, Lindsey Fire Chief Tom Overmyer said.

The family, of ~~3402 Sandusky County Road 270~~, got back from church about 11:15 a.m. to find their kitchen table on fire and

Think of that. What are the odds on the whole family catching fire at the same time?

32 ignorant enough to serve on North jury

WASHINGTON — After four days of questioning prospective jurors, the judge and lawyers in Oliver North's Iran-Contra trial are learning that even in this news hub there are people who do not care about what is happening.

By the end of Friday's session, U.S. District Judge Gerhard A. Gesell declared 24 women and eight men ignorant enough of North's 1987

Here's a headline that pretty much says it all.

Braille dictionary for sale. Must see to appreciate!

Call Jerry

LEGAL NOTICE

NOTICE OF TRUSTEE'S SALE

I

NOTICE IS HEREBY GIVEN that the undersigned Trustee will on the 16th day of October, 1987, at the hour of 9:00 o'clock a.m., at the Wetmore Entrance Snohomish County Courthouse, in the City of Everett, State of Washington, sell at public auction to the highest and best bidder, payable at the time of sale, the following described real property, situated in the county of Snohomish State of Washington, to wit:

The north half of the southwest quarter of the southwest quarter, the north half of the northeast quarter of the southwest quarter of the southwest quarter of the southwest quarter, the southeast quarter of the southwest quarter of the southwest quarter and that portion of the northwest quarter of the southeast quarter of the southwest quarter lying westerly of the center line of that certain easement recorded under Recording Number 2246421, all in Section 33, Township 31 North, Range 5 East, W.M., in Snohomish County, Washington;

EXCEPT the west 40 feet of the north

Think a lawyer wrote this one?

CHARITY BAZAAR

SATURDAY & SUNDAY ONLY!
Support Our Salina Area Clubs
And Organizations
- Baked Goods
- Craft Items
- Ticket Sales
- And More!

AND

Don't Miss the United Way Celebration!

Activities and Demonstrations All Day
Saturday and Sunday — <u>Including a Child Choking
Training Program</u> Saturday at 2:00 p.m.

Come Join The Fun!

That pretty much takes care of your baby-sitting problem.

From the "We've got to destroy this village to save it" department:

City Increasing Speed Limit to Slow Down Drivers

POWDER SPRINGS

The Powder Springs City Council Monday increased the speed limit on three city streets from 25 to 35 miles per hour, but delayed a decision on whether to raise the speed limit on Brownsville Road. Action on the

Organ expert impressed by ones here

By Staff Writer

When it comes to organs, we in Helena just don't know how good we've got it.

So it *is* size and not technique that counts.

● **First Annual Animal Abuse Council Benefit Pig Roast**, ▓▓▓▓▓▓. 9 a.m. trail ride (bring your own horse), 2 p.m. Pig Roast, Saturday, American Ozarks Campground, Highway 86 and JJ, Blue

Keep totally current with these titles in

Infectious Disease

You can try them FREE!

Swap 'em. Trade 'em with your friends.
Collect the whole set.

CORRECTION

The China Seafood
Restaurant ad
that ran in last Tuesday's
Pennysaver/News
was incorrect.
It read
中国飲輯茶室
It should have read
店飯鮮海国中
We regret any
inconvenience this
may have caused.

I thought there was
something funny
the first time I saw that.

Ban On Nude Dancing On Governor's Desk

ATLANTA (AP) — Gov. Joe Frank Harris' signature is the only step remaining to ban nude dancing in bars in Georgia.

Harris has said he would "look favorably" at the bill, which would take effect immediately upon his signature.

The idea's six-year journey through the Legislature ended Thursday when the Senate voted 44-7 to prohibit liquor license holders from offering live nude dancing or films depicting nudity or simulated sex acts.

The bill includes detailed definitions of impermissible nudity which apparently could not be

THE 1988 GEORGIA LEGISLATURE

belt bill by next week.

—The Senate Education Committee approved a bill to require sex education in all public schools, but it added a provision allowing parents to remove their children from such classes.

But what you do in your house is your business.

Organ recital fades after firm beginning

Organist Frederick Swann made his name at posh churches of Chicago and Manhattan before heading west to Robert Schuller's Crystal Cathedral in Southern California, where he plays the organ and directs the music program.

Monday night, appearing in recital at Southwestern Baptist Theological Seminary in Fort Worth, he performed a program concentrating on romantic and mainstream 20th-century organ music.

Swann put his best foot forward first, with a radiant rendition of French com-

Tell me about it.

"I hope they found nothing wrong" department:

Building burns to the ground following safety inspection

Town of Pewaukee — A fire inspector was forced to flee a building he had just finished inspecting Thursday when the structure caught fire and burned to the ground.

Cows 'perform' to benefit ballet troupe

Valley Photo, Bill Noble

~~Jay Leno~~ gives puzzled look to Yuma ballerinas and their cow, which will do its 'dancing' Saturday

Okay, so it's not New York, but...

10

Everyone is familiar with Mark Twain's famous quote, "The reports of my death have been greatly exaggerated." It just goes to show, the more things change, the more they remain the same. That's why we've entitled this chapter:

SORRY, OUR RECORDS SHOW YOU'RE DEAD

Ohio man, 79, pronounced dead, but says he feels much better now

Tax return may be required after death

May be required? Could I find out now
so I can rest in peace?

Man's 'serious' condition an improvement over death

Associated Press

KNOXVILLE — ~~Bishop Thomas Dupont~~ was listed in serious condition Sunday at Park West Hospital — but he's in better shape than earlier when he was declared dead.

Wait till he gets the bill. He might change his mind.

It's official: Dead people can't vote

AUGUSTA — After 22 years answering last-minute election questions from city and town clerks, ███████████ didn't bat an eye Monday when a caller asked her if the dead can vote.

"Some lady voted absentee Saturday and died Sunday," ████ explained later as she recalled the query. "Can they count the ballot?"

I guess this reporter never lived in Chicago.

Death row inmates no longer allowed day off after execution, official says

Boy, you thought the other warden was tough.

Auditor says college enrolled dead people

██████████ — (UPI) — ██████ ████ Junior College officials may have registered dead students and misclassified hundreds of nursing home residents to increase registration figures and obtain more state money, a preliminary audit says.

I think I was in some of those classes.

'Butcher of Balkans' dies

BELGRADE, Yugoslavia—Andrija Artukovic, who was extradited from the United States and convicted of ordering thousands of prisoners killed in World War II, has died in jail at the age of 88.

Known as the "Butcher of the Balkans," Artukovic had been sentenced to death by firing squad in May 1986, but his execution had been postponed indefinitely because of his ill health.

Death may ease tension

PORT-AU-PRINCE, Haiti (UPI) — Diplomats say the death of Col. Jean-Claude Paul, a suspected drug trafficker who died after eating what police believe was poisoned pumpkin soup, may help ease tensions between the United States and Haiti.

Yeah, but what if it doesn't!

Woman dead when head removed

UWM theater training dead for '88

I guess they must need more help at the Motor Vehicles Bureau.

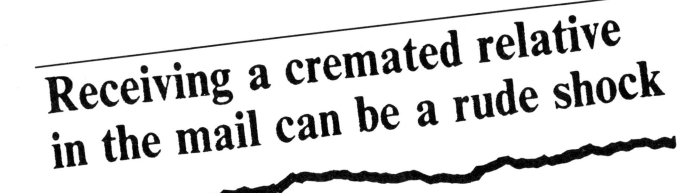

Receiving a cremated relative in the mail can be a rude shock

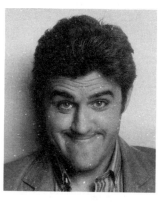

Hey, Ma, Grandpa's back!

Funny, WM seeks enthusiastic aud. for headline bk.
Must enjoy reading about plane crashes, condoms, and
people who aren't really dead. No weirdos, please.

SPEAKING PERSONALLY

Oh why did you have to die and leave this Earth so early? Every day I grieve that you are no longer with us. This message dedicated to my wife's first husband.

M.H.L.

MERV'S MOWERS

Merv. is out of jail now & back at his shop in 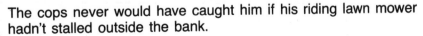. He welcomes all of his old customers. For honest mower repairs, call

The cops never would have caught him if his riding lawn mower hadn't stalled outside the bank.

NEVER MARRIED WHITE MALE—Honest, gentle, affectionate, widely traveled college professor-writer, PhD, seeks spiritual, intelligent, gentle female age 40-50 for a meaningful relationship. I am heterosexual and enjoy jazz, metaphysics, <u>dressing as a woman</u>, and dining out. Write to: Box H-3, c/o

Jazz? Who likes jazz?

"Ads that speak for themselves" department:

MUST SELL: Health food store, due to failing health. 1-8

"Do you think this guy watches Donahue?" department:

FARMER LOOKING FOR
WIFE WITH TRACTOR
If interested, please send
picture of tractor: P. O. Box
2518,

"You show me yours, I'll show mine" department:

NOTICE TO ANYONE wishing to go to Van Wert, Dec. 12, for hernia operation, contact ~~Mary~~

LOST DONALD DUCK WALLET -
Need for identification. Please call. ~~telephone~~.

If you find it, please call Vice President Dan Quayle immediately.

Will swap white satin wedding gown (worn once) for 50 pounds fresh Gravy Train.

Sure, she's got a big appetite but she's cheap to feed.

MOVING SALE - Wheel-chair, hospital bed, deluxe sliding chair stair glide, and a motorcycle.

Gosh, I wonder what happened.

Babysitter - Looking for infant to babysit in my home. Excellent references.

Young man, 20, wants job on stud farm w/rm., prefer to work for a lady. ~~Reynolds~~, Box 87134, **College Park** 30337. ~~~~ aft. 6 p.m.

Nice work if you can get it.

NEED BABYSITTER at my home, bring own lunch and dinner. Stay until I get home. 6:15 a.m. until whenever. No overtime pay. Call ~~6_____8~~.

Ask for Ebeneazar.

Town of South Hadley: An equal opportunity employer. Reliable person needed to remove dead animals on public roadways. Persons interested contact South Hadley Board of Health at ███-████.

Gee, a once in a lifetime opportunity to enter the high-paying world of carcas removal.

510 Help Wanted

VACANCY for a part-time Breastfeeding Coordinator. 20 hours/week, $6.50/hour. Looking for organized person with public relation, teaching and record-keeping skills. Breastfeeding Experience preferred, but not required.

Coordinator? You're pretty much limited to two choices, aren't you?

NEED Plain Clothes Security. Must have shop lifting experience. Apply between 8a.m.-3p.m. Mon.-Fri., at ————— —————— ——————, suite 207.

Hmmm...murder, burglary, assault...Sorry, we're looking for someone with shoplifting experience.

600-General

AIR TRAFFIC CONTROL. FAA accepting applications now. $24,000 - $62,000. No aviation experience necessary. All day exam preparation course.

At least at the other job you had to have some shoplifting experience.

SURGICAL ASSISTANT

NO EXP NEC. Execl career opp'ty for a bright, dependable person who likes people. We will train you in our busy Mt Kisco Oral surgery office. Salary & benefits open

I hear this is the job you get if you're turned down as a security guard or air traffic controller.

Gorbachev launching glasnost? Oprah losing 67 pounds?
Pee Wee Herman a movie star?

WHO WOULDA THOUGHT?

Iran severs relations with Iran

Even *they* don't like themselves!

In the sewers, each day's job has new allure

Charcoal briquettes destroyed by fire

Associated Press

ELK GROVE, Calif. — Fire broke out in a warehouse containing more than 1,000 tons of charcoal briquettes, authorities said.

It had to be arson. Do you know how hard it is to light those stupid briquettes?

13

Advertising is big business in this country. Companies spend a fortune doing market research, demographic surveys, psychological profiles—all in an effort to make their product seem different from the competition's. Well, the products you'll see in this next group of advertisements certainly are. That's why we call this chapter:

YOU'RE SELLING WHAT?

Kids Are Grreat Meals

Packed in novelty cartons with surprise. All meals include beverage.

Buy One And Get One FREE!

with this coupon Good Through 2/29/88

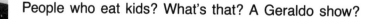

People who eat kids? What's that? A Geraldo show?

(156)

9-VOLT SMOKE ALARM WITH SILENCER

Model 105/742-49

Yeah, the last thing you need is this thing waking you up in the middle of the night, huh?

PICTORIAL DENTURE
(A COMBINATION OF DENTAL TECHNOLOGY AND PHOTOGRAPHIC ART)

This invention has been developed for identification and transformation of the tiresome task of constructing dentures into a pleasant artistic process.

The upper denture contains a transparent color picture which will remain intact for the life of the denture.

Be thankful these people are doing dental work and not proctology!

You can learn to dance like a Contra

This is the first time a class for learning contras has been offered at Leisure World. What is a contra? A contra is almost literally a dance of opposition. It is usually performed by many couples, face to face, line facing line, in long lines normally formed lengthwise of the hall, so that the head of the line is at the caller's end of the hall. It is becom-

HONEYBAKED HAM

O.J.'S FAVORITE HOLIDAY MEAL

O.J., that's not a ham, it's a turkey.
If anyone should know a pigskin, it should be O.J.

"Hey, this dog is dented" department:

McComb Supply's Annual
CAT & DOG SALE!
SCRATCHED & DENTED ITEMS

SALE STARTS
MARCH 2nd & 3rd
Thurs. & Fri.
From
7:30 A.M.
TO
4:30 P.M.

ALL FLOOR SAMPLES
10% OFF
(EXCEPT APPLIANCES & T.V.s)

REGISTERED MINIATURE American Eskimos, females-$150, male-$125. Ready to go.

Buy two. Keep them in the freezer.

"Eat quick before it escapes" department:

Mr. A's UPTOWN

Seafood, Live Pasta & Creole
FREE – HALF PRICE – 20% off Etc.
We honor any
Restaurant Coupon
Good for Lunch or Dinner
*Same coupon restrictions apply
Selected Special Entrees Excluded.
Dine in Only. 1 coupon per couple.
15% gratuity will be added before discount.
6396 Richmond ● 780-FOOD
OPEN SUNDAYS
SUPER BOWL PARTY - SUNDAY
Happy Hour – Free Snacks

Harper's Boneless Old-Fashioned Pit Barbeque. Old fashioned microwaveable package. Warm up for a delicious   Sandwich in a minute
#711 . . 2 to 3 lbs. avg. $12.25

Old-fashioned microwave? Remember Grandma's day when it took up to *three* minutes to microwave a package?

**#T1758 WINDPROOF PANEL
BRIEF $15.50**
(Please specify size)

G

Windproof
Panel

Windproof? If it wasn't for the wind,
this guy wouldn't get any action at all.

MUST SELL!
3 grave spaces in Laureland, very reasonable. Plus air-conditioner.

If you get the plot next to the air conditioner, it would be a good place to use the windproof underwear.

"If rabbit feet were lucky, they'd still be on the rabbit" department:

RABBIT fur coat, size medium $45. Small hutch, $55.

Flu doesn't take a holiday, and neither do we!

At Memorial Community Hospital we realize that you can get sick at any time. That's why we offer convenient medical care at both Health Branch West and at our Emergency Trauma Center throughout the year.

Our Emergency Trauma Center is open 365 days a year,
24 hours a day,
so you can get medical care when you need it throughout the holidays.

Health Branch West Holiday Hours
behind Hy-Vee, next to Capital Mall

9 a.m.-7 p.m.   Noon-6 p.m.
Monday-Saturday   Sunday

CLOSED THANKSGIVING DAY
No Appointment Necessary

Professional and personal care where you live and work.

MEMORIAL COMMUNITY HOSPITAL

Better not choke on that turkey...

This last chapter is one of my favorites. I can understand how, under the pressure of deadlines, a misplaced word or ungrammatical sentence can slip by, but when a picture is placed next to a headline, you assume the two are related and when you find out they're not, well, it makes you wonder. Impossible, you say? How could that happen?

PICTURE THIS

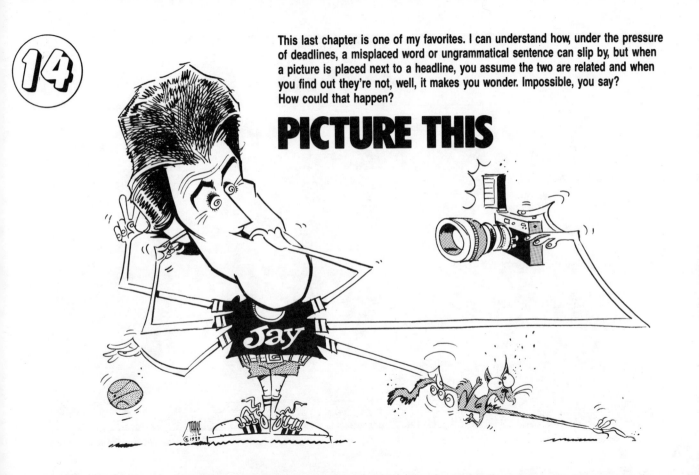

Living

Manuel Dias, The Modesto Bee

One body in yard identified

SACRAMENTO, Calif. (AP) — One of the seven bodies found buried outside a boardinghouse was identified as that of an alcoholic who spent most of his life on the streets, but authorities don't know how he or the others died.

The body of Benjamin Fink, 60, a former resident of Dorothea Puente's boardinghouse in downtown Sacramento, was identified Monday through

AP/Wide World Photos

Dirty job

President and Mrs. Reagan shovel dirt at the groundbreaking ceremony for the Reagan Presidential Library in Simi Valley, Calif., Monday.

"This shine's going to cost you a little extra" department:

Jerry Daul, center, Dennis DeGrusha, left, and Mayor Ronnie Harris stand in front of the newly restored Jefferson Memorial.
STAFF PHOTO BY JIM SIGMON

Jeff war memorial basks in glow of community's effort

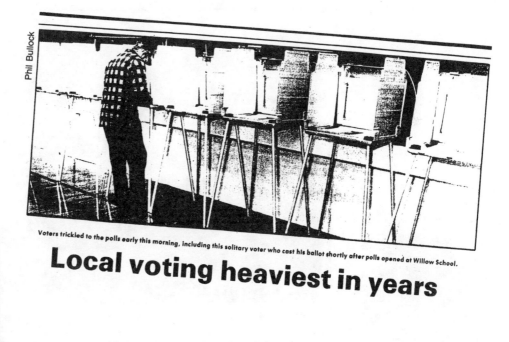

Voters trickled to the polls early this morning, including this solitary voter who cast his ballot shortly after polls opened at Willow School.

Local voting heaviest in years

Looks like it's going to be a close race.

The Arizona Republic, Doyle Sanders

DEADLY CAST / State Game and Fish Department personnel spray rotenone, a poison that kills only fish and some aquatic insects, into a Lake Pleasant cove. The department earlier this week said killing all the fish in three coves is the most accurate method of determining the lake's fish population. They added that the poison poses no danger to swimmers or water skiers.

Now, if they don't kill every fish, will it still be accurate?

"Has Jimmy Swaggart heard about this?" department:

AP/Wide World Photos

Seduction costly for ex-pastor

Associated Press

TACOMA, Wash. — A woman who sued her former pastor for seducing her has been awarded $130,000 by a jury, a verdict intended partly as a warning to other ministers.

"We want the community to see that this can't keep happening," juror Cathy Zurfluh said Friday. "It's got to stop somewhere."

The Topeka Capital-Journal

Heading for national

The Jefferson County 4-H meat judging team, winners in the Kansas state contest Aug. 27 in Emporia, practiced in a Topeka grocery this past week for the

Team members are, from left, ~~~~~~~~~~ Valley Falls veterinaria

No comment.

The El Reno Tribune

Moslem extremists renew threats against hostages

BEIRUT, Lebanon (AP) — Shiite Moslem extremists holding U.S. hostages repeated their long-standing demands for the Americans' release in a new statement, threatening reprisal if the demands are not met.

— Uh oh

"It's time to modernize the forces" department:

U.S. troops going to Honduras

WASHINGTON (AP) — About 3,200 American infantry and airborne troops are flying to Honduras today in the most dramatic show of U.S. force in the six-year Nicaraguan war, causing the Senate's top Democrat to accuse President Reagan of "overreaction."

The White House described the movement as "an emergency deployment readiness exercise" triggered by what it called the invasion of Honduras by 1,500 to 2,000 Nicaraguan forces pursuing Contra rebels.

The exercise involves two battalions of the 82nd Airborne Division from Fort Bragg, N.C., and two battalions from the 7th Infantry Division at Fort Ord, Calif.

The troops will be posted out of harm's way for an indefinite period near the Palmerola Air Force Base in Honduras, about 125 miles from the area of reported hostilities, said Marlin Fitzwater, the president's spokesman.

"This exercise is a measured response designed to show our staunch support to the democratic government of Honduras at a time when its territorial integrity is being violated by the Cuban- and Soviet-supported Sandinista army," Fitzwater said in a late-night announcement.

He said it also was "a signal to the governments and peoples of Central America of the seriousness with which the United States government views the current situation in the region."

Some congressional Democrats weren't buying the administration's rationale.

"It's an overreaction," said Senate Majority Leader Robert Byrd, D-W.Va. "The Sandinistas have crossed over the border before and gone back."

"I just hope it's merited," Sen. John Kerry, D-Mass., said, recalling a similar incident two years ago when the United States jumped to the aid of Honduras under circumstances many saw as exaggerated by the White

(See TROOPS, page 12)

Monroe Evening Times

Juveniles recaptured in Bacliff

BACLIFF — Two juveniles who escaped from a youth group home in Galveston Thursday and threatened to shoot a police officer were apprehended around 6 p.m. that day, according to a Galveston County Sheriff's Department spokeswoman.

Reports show the two youths and a companion escaped from the home sometime Thursday morning and were discovered inside a Bacliff residence around noon by a police officer. The spokeswoman said she did not know which law enforcement department the officer was from.

. The officer left the house to wait for assistance after the juveniles raised a shotgun and threatened to kill him, the spokeswoman said. By the time the backup officers arrived, the juveniles had left the home.

One of the youths was captured a short time later about two blocks from the house. The other two led officers on a five-hour chase in which a DPS helicopter and several other vehicles were utilized, reports indicate.

The youths were apprehended around 6 p.m. at the end of 16th Street.

All three juveniles were charged

SEE JUVENILES, PAGE 2

AP/Wide World Photos

HARE-RAISING VISIT — Thomas Phillips, 9 months, and Sharell Phillips, 2, of Allentown, Pa., didn't much enjoy their visit with the Easter Bunny at a mall Friday.

If you want to catch a criminal, you have to think like a criminal...

(179)

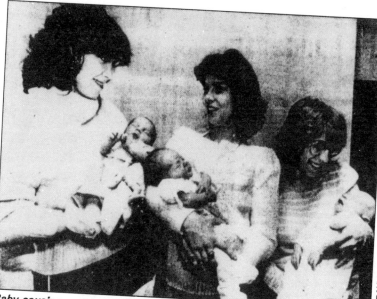

Baby cousins

These Chattanooga-area sisters all had babies a day apart to finish out 1986. From left are ⬛⬛⬛ with son, ⬛⬛⬛, born on Dec. 29; ⬛⬛⬛ with son, ⬛⬛⬛, born Dec. 31; and ⬛⬛⬛ with daughter, ⬛⬛⬛, born Dec. 30. (AP Photo)

Former affair's result has grown too big for this couple to ignore

Does Steve Garvey know about this?

Americans are eating way to grave

WASHINGTON (AP) — Millions of Americans are waddling their way to early graves by consuming too much fat, too much salt and washing it all down with too much booze, the U.S. surgeon general reported on Wednesday.

"Diseases of dietary excess and imbalance" are among the leading causes of death in the United States, said the report issued by C. Everett Koop. "Over-consumption ... is now a major concern for Americans."

The study said that of 2.1 million Americans who died last year, nearly 1.5 million succumbed to diseases associated with diet.

"What we eat may affect our risk for several of the leading causes of death for Americans, notably coronary heart disease, stroke, atherosclerosis, diabetes, and some types of cancer," the report said. "These disorders together now account for more than two-thirds of all deaths in the United States."

The study said that many Americans are too fat, while others fail to get required nutrients such as calcium and iron. And the report repeatedly emphasized the need to cut down on consumption of animal products and replace them with a greater variety of foods, particularly fruits, vegetables and whole grains.

Nutrition experts praised the report, predicting that may have an important impact on how Americans regard their diet and on products sold by the food industry.

Charles J. Carey, president of the National Food Processors Association, said the report will encourage companies to develop products that follow the guidelines endorsed in the report.

Though the report acknowledges that malnutrition remains a problem in some parts of the world and for certain Americans, it says that "for most of us the more likely problem has become one of overeating — too many calories for our activity levels and an imbalance in the nutrients

Bedford Gazette

"If you miss class, we'll hold you under" department:

AP/Wide World Photos

A police officer and a resident wade through floodwaters in the town of Uribia on Wednesday after Hurricane Joan hit the Colombian coast.

Classes to help public spot 'fishy' seafood

Staff Writer

TALLAHASSEE — Declaring that "the best inspectors in the world are an educated public," members of Florida's fishing industry on Wednesday announced a series of seminars aimed at teaching consumers how to spot problem seafood.

The fish dealers and industry lobbyists staged a news conference to announce that they hope to ease public concerns over recent outbreaks of seafood-related illnesses and revelations of fish fraud, including the deliberate substitution of inexpensive fillets for popular catches such as grouper and red snapper.

"The seafood business, just like any other business, has its good and its bad," said Mike Abrams, owner of Captain Mike's seafood stores in Hallandale and Fort Lauderdale. "We think the good far outweighs the bad."

Standing before an elaborate display of fresh seafood, Robert Jones, executive director of the Tallahassee-based Southeastern Fisheries Association, said: "These are legitimate and bona fide fishermen who see their businesses diminishing. They feel there is another side to the story."

Jones said the majority of fishermen

SEE **FISH** / 15A

"I feel like I'm wearing nothing at all" department:

AP/Wide World Photos

New devices jolt, restart hearts of cardiac victims

The Associated Press

BOSTON — New devices that automatically deliver heart-starting electrical jolts and can be operated with little training could save many of the 400,000 Americans who die each year of cardiac arrest, according to a new report.

Quality time

Honeymoon Stephen enjoy the shade of the trees — and the company of their grandson, Phillip Baxter, 6 — at Fenton City Park recently.

Brad Hohenstreet photo.

Some kids *demand* quality time and get it.

**"Lock up your daughters"
department:**

John J. Watkins

WEENIE WAGON: A peculiar sight rolled down Cine Ave. in Griffith Tuesday. It was none other than the Oscar Mayer Wiener Mobile stopping to get gassed up at a local gas station.

Sex education requires parents

185

FAA examining airlines' mechanical problems

DETROIT — The Federal Aviation Administration has quietly begun its first system-wide look at the mechanical problems of airplanes in daily service, according to federal officials.

cut back on the margin of safety by letting items go unrepaired for days at a time.

They say the airline industry's deregulation and intense competition has spurred cost-cutting carriers to put off repairs, trim maintenance facilities and lower their spare parts inventories.

The FAA's probe of a dozen of the nation's major airlines, which began on Aug. 10, is expected to last several months. Agency officials here and at other FAA facilities in Washington and across the country said the survey was not triggered by any specific complaint or event.

Air Line Pilots Association with prompting the federal action.

They also note that T. Allan McArtor, who became the FAA's administrator in July, has spoken of the MELS at recent meetings with aviation groups, indicating a concern about their impact on airplane safety.

Takeoff position

████████████, 7, is stretched out in flying form as he tries out his skateboard on a newly paved parking lot in downtown Adrian, Mich.

Looks a little tail heavy to me.

EXCELLENT OUTLOOK — After receiving a broken neck in an accident, John Peck, staying at the Prescott Veterans Administration Medical Center, was tired of all the sad and sympathetic looks he was getting from passers-by. Peck decided to put the American flags on to his neck brace and now he says " people smile when they walk by."

He dreams of Mars visit

Many years ago, when he was just eight, Brian O'Leary conceived his dream: "Let's go to Mars."

It's 1988, much time has passed and O'Leary has gone through some of life's passages, but his vision is still intact...only now greatly expanded. He wants the United States to join with Russia in a 1999 mission to Mars to herald in the millenium as an affirmation of world peace and unity.

To do this, he would scrap the Star Wars program, "a system that will not work," and put that money and work force toward going to the Red Planet and into other programs that would enrich the human condition.

The former astronaut, educator

You know, I think he'll make it.

PROHIBITED
PEDESTRIANS
BICYCLES
MOTOR SCOOTERS
METAL TREADS
FARM IMPLEMENTS
ANIMALS ON FOOT

Rita Cichowlas, Cin. O.